RELATIVITY THEORY OF BEINGS

AND

HOLINESS, THE ULTIMATE FORM OF LEADERSHIP

RELATIVITY THEORY OF BEINGS

AND

HOLINESS, THE ULTIMATE FORM OF LEADERSHIP

by

Theodore T. Noonchester Jr.
Illustrations by the Author

This book is dedicated to All Beings the World Over

Table of Contents

Preface

There are some academics that believe that there no longer exists such a thing as an original thought or idea, that all original thoughts and ideas have already been thought of and documented over the past thousands of years of recorded history. With the possible exception of the advanced sciences odds are against a 21st century idea to be original and not to have been predicated in some form or another sometime in the past. (Sullivan, 2002) The death of original thoughts (especially in the field of philosophy) leave present day scholars with little to do but argue over meanings and interpretations of old ideas.

The field of philosophy dealing with being or existence is called ontology (Wikipedia, 2007) and has been studied for thousands of years. Theories of Beings, theories about beings, or what it means to be a being, have been contemplated and postulated by many of the world's greatest philosophers (Aristotle, Plato, Aquinas, Nietzsche, Sartre, Descartes, Kant and more).

With that qualification this Relativity Theory of Beings is a documentation of observations that may (probably) had been observed and documented, at least in part, in some form or fashion at some time over the last 2000+ years.

When finished with this book the reader should begin to see the myriad of ways and places Relativity Theory of Beings fits with the world. The billions of the world's individuals each belongs to some extent or another to relatively greater beings than themselves. Be it families, clans, cults, religions communities, nations, races, groups, clubs, teams, philosophies, political parties…the list can reach into the hundreds…

It's the authors' intent to follow up this book with a much expanded book on the same subject that goes into much greater detail and offer suggestions on how to deal with some of the problems faced between beings.

Introduction

Relativity Theory of Beings is a model that can be used to describe and illustrate beings in all their myriad of forms. It can be applied to define fundamental philosophical questions, many of which philosophers have pondered and quarreled for thousands of years…questions such as what is good? What is bad? What is Holy? And what is evil?

This "Relativity" Theory of Beings began as an attempt to figure out God and humanities purpose in the universe. Many believe that one of the prime goals for humanity is to figure out or to know God. This stems from a logic path that begins for many as searching for reasons and purpose for their own lives:

Many people wake in the morning not particularly ambitious wondering

"Why am I getting up?"

"Why do I go to work? to pay the bills? To Support my family?"

"Is there something more?"

"Why was I put on this earth?"

"Why was anyone put on this earth?"

"Why was I even created?"

"If there is a Creator, what did the Creator intend to create during creation?"

Understanding God brings people closer to God and helps to elevate humanity to a higher level than it had existed before (Ayatullah Murtada Mutahhari, 2007). To know God and understand humanities purpose in the universe is in itself almost god like.

The fear of pride has caused many to consider it impossible or sacrilegious to even attempt to know

God. In the Judeo-Christian story of the tower of Babel, God confuses mankind with many languages and destroys the tower a united mankind was building to reach the heavens. Another example is the story of Job; Job was a saintly man who is made to suffer great adversities at the hands of Satan. When Job demands audience with God in order to argue the reasons for the many adversities wrought down upon him, God grants audience but Job is overwhelmed by the presence of God and is silenced. (Job 40:4)

Greek Gods are well known for trying to keep mankind subservient. Plato describes a time when there existed powerful humans that were both man and woman with four arms and legs. These super humans conspired on how to ascend to the heavens.

The Gods became upset and Zeus decided to weaken the super humans by splitting them in half. Once split the super humans no longer aspired for the heavens. This was viewed by many as drastic, even among the gods, so Zeus showed compassion and allowed the much diminished humans the ability to find their soul mate.

God's in general demand unquestioning obedience; history is littered with stories and fables that highlight that point. Yet a fool that is willing to attempt the impossible will have an infinitely better chance of success than the wise that never tries.

Brainstorming a list of God related questions (God, singular - assuming monotheism, in order to restrict the scope and be able to put a box around what otherwise would be a limitless question) yields questions like; what is God? What are humans? How are people and God the same? How are people and God different? To figure out these questions it is prudent to divide the problem into smaller more manageable parts.

One of the most obvious differences between human kind and God is that God doesn't have a physical human form (the Christian belief in Jesus not withstanding). God doesn't have a physical body, yet most would agree that God is a being (Edwards, 1998).

God is a being and people are "human" beings, which in turn may be broken down into simpler terms. Taking away the human portion from "human beings" leaves beings. The question now becomes what is a human being without a "human" body. Put another way what is a human being without the needs wants and desires related to the physical or animal form? Take away thirst, hunger, the need for shelter, lust…take away all need. Take away the flesh, strip people of their humanity and what is left? For some the answer would assuredly be nothing, many people are totally controlled by the need to satisfy the needs, wants and desires of the body (flesh).

The premise that physical needs take priority is the basis of Maslow's famous hierarchy of needs. The idea is like that of the pyramid with physiological and safety needs at the lower levels that take precedence over the higher social/ego-status/self-actualization or non-physical needs. The lower portions of the Maslow's needs deal exclusively with the needs of the flesh and need to be fulfilled before other needs become important. (Thinkers, 1999)

Maslow's hierarchy of needs

What separates humans from the rest of the animals that roam the earth? What makes people better than dogs, cats, pigs or any other animal? For that matter, what makes humans any better than plants or insects or any other life form on the planet? Taken to an extreme what makes a living human being different than someone that is brain dead or in a non-responsive coma or even cold flesh lying on a mortuary slab? When the question is isolated down to the most basic of questions, answers begin to form. To move flesh there must be life, beyond live there must be control to sustain that life. Beyond control driven by the need to sustain life, humans have discretionary or "relatively" more control than plants and animals.

This discretionary control has enabled mankind to make great achievements, but for what purpose? Beyond control needed to sustain life, the original questions reappear; and those are, what is mankind's purpose? What was God's purpose when creating mankind? To answer these questions it is important to put them into context and one way to establish parameters around a question is though limits. The Ultimate limits on mankind's existence deal with life and death.

Death is inevitable, and an individual's life represents a very small portion of the world as a whole. In the grand scheme of things we spend most of eternity either not conceived of yet or dead. What is the importance of a person's life if it is only one of 6 billion alive today or represents less than a millionth of the span of life on the earth and what of the universe? Compared to the universe and to eternity the life of a single individual is nothing.

The job of giving meaning to our existence and gain purpose for our lives has been fulfilled (or attempted to be fulfilled) by many religions. Even some philosophers believe themselves tasked with finding norms or guidelines for mankind to more or less live by. (Horowitz, 1998) Without meaning or purpose there would be little or no order to human civilization, chaos would rule and mankind would not have advanced much beyond the level of animals.

The difference between the nonexistence before life and the non-existence after death (at least in the physical world) is that we were here and a fortunate few leave an effect or mark that remains in the physical world after we die. This mark or lasting effect left on the world is how we are judged.

What was accomplished during a persons life is what the survivors of the deceased use to evaluate the life. The value of the activities and accomplishments of life is especially true for those that believe in an after life and final judgment. This places enormous value on what we accomplish with our lives and the impressions we make on those left living.

Being

The level of control that enables mankind to make lasting impressions on the world and other beings differentiates mankind from the rest of the life on earth. Using control as the core of a model for a being, the next logical and observed element to be added is that what cannot be controlled can be influenced. Beyond influence what cannot be influenced is known, beyond knowledge, what is not known is aware of. Finally what is not even aware of is the unknown. A being can be described as a core of control followed by layers (extending out like that of an onion) of influence, knowledge, awareness and unknown.

A being can now be defined as control, influence, knowledge and awareness, unknown is the universe beyond. Control, influence, knowledge and awareness are without flesh and our mastery of these elements divides us from animals. Yet much of the control a being has is over the flesh, it is our connection to the physical world.

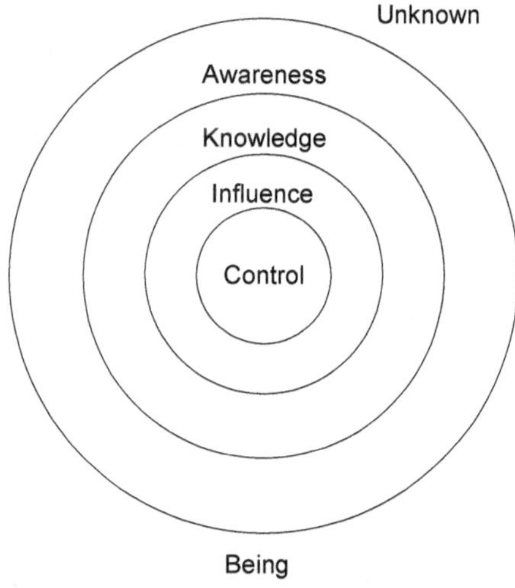

Control and influence is strongly linked to knowledge. Knowledge is power (Buchanan, 2006), control without knowledge (or knowledge without purpose) is chaos.

All beings have these elements, from plants and animals to space aliens and Gods. Animals are largely motivated by their physical/bodily needs or instincts and do to some extent have control beyond pure instinct. (Bernard & Mills & Swenson, & Walsh, 2005) Animals have the ability to recognize and interact with each other and with humans. They have been known to perform acts of self sacrifice that some debate would not have occurred had they been driven by pure instinct. Other scientists argue that even animal self sacrifice can be attributed to genes. (Papineau, 1998) The acts of plants and insects on the other hand seem to be governed solely on biological or instinctual basis. (Trewavas, 2003)

What differentiates beings is the different or "relative" levels of control, influence, knowledge and awareness each has and the body that houses them. The body is the medium through which the being exerts control and influence on the world and the body is also the medium through which the world interacts with the being.

What makes an individual is a combination of knowledge, experiences and body. Given the same knowledge, the same experiences and the same body, any two persons would be the same. This has significant and dramatic consequences. It means that all people are the same. Each person if born into another person's body, and having the same experiences, and gaining the same knowledge, would be that other person. This means that one person looking into the eyes of another person, should be able to see themselves. Had it not been for fate or the act of some divine being, each person could have been the other. The adage that People should treat each other as they would treat themselves gains new relevance because all beings really <u>are</u> the same.

The universe, nature, religious divinity or God is the ultimate entity or being that dominates the universe, having control, influence, knowledge and awareness of everything that lesser beings do not. Relatively lesser beings like humans are patterned in the same way as Gods having control, influence, knowledge and awareness and obtain (or are given) some control as they come into the universe and grow. Gods and people are therefore patterned from the same mold -- beings.

Human beings control can be differentiated by what motivates it, philosophers, psychologists and sociologists have come to some agreement on internal vs. external elements of human capacity. They have identified two basic categories of knowledge and motivating factors:

Of this earth - external	not of this earth – internal
Intrinsic values	extrinsic values (Zimmerman, 2002)
Nominal essences	real essences (Wigelsworth, 2003)
Hygiene factors	motivators Herzberg's Two Factor Theory (Swierczek, 1988)

Lower levels of motivatoin	higher levels of motivation Maslow's hierarchy of needs (Thinkers, 1999)
Rationally self-interested	rational moral agents (Sugden, 2004)
Being-for-itself	being in-itself (Gardner, 2006)
The visible	the invisible (Morley, 2005)
Knowledge of World	Knowledge of reason – Plato

The ability to recognize "I" as an entity is subtle proof of our ability to see ourselves from a perspective not of this earth. Andre Descartes' famous "I think therefore I am" (Newman, 2005) points to this fact and hints that our true existance is not of this earth.

The distinction between of this earth and not of this earth can also be used as a method of separating human beings from lesser beings and animals or even between human beings themselves.

Throughout history many people and peoples have attemped to raise their existiance above the physical (of this earth) to a higher level (not of this earth) in an attempt to clean or purify themselves of animal ways and to become closer to God. (Miller, 1996) Vows of self denial are common among the holy persons of many religions. Hindu and Buddhist monks, Christian priests, and devout Muslims are but a few examples of pious individuals that often live a life of isolation, poverty or celibacy. Some of these devout individuals even sacrifice their lives in martyrdom based on a belief of life outside of earthly existence. The goal of these people is to distance or separate themselves from the physical world and live closer to or in the spiritual world of God.

The realm of God is not of this earth, which places Gods existence at the knowledge of reason level, rather than the knowledge of the world level as described by Plato. God is ranked at a higher level and is cleaner due to the non connectedness to the physical world. The distinction between of this earth and not of this earth has created many moral and spiritual conflicts that various philosophies, ideologies and religions have attempted to resolve.

Many people feel a strong desire even a need to be close to God. An all powerful God that is perfect beyond comprehension creates for some people an alien God that they have trouble accepting.

Jesus who is viewed by Christians as the son of God bridges the god/man gap and enables Christians to think of God as having first hand understanding of the human condition alowing them to feel closer to God.

Knowing what we are is only part of the question of what our purpose is in the universe. Another philosophical question that has been around for thousands of years deals with good and bad. Goodness and badness relates to the question of mankind's purpose. A simple solution to the problem of mankind's purpose is to do good. But what is good?

What is good?

The field of philosophy that deals with the question of good and bad is ethics. Ethics deals with goodness and badness and what is right and wrong.

Good has had many descriptions over the millennia but seems to have settled around ideas such as perfection and intrinsic good. Good is sometimes described as "perfect". (Wall, 2007) A perfect being is one that which fits exactly with nature or its surroundings. (Johnson, 2000) Intrinsic Good or value is often defined as something that has value "for its own sake" or "in itself". (Zimmerman, 2002) There are many other definitions of good but in order to limit the scope of this book the focus will be on what is good for a being using the model of control, influence, knowledge and awareness

(Relativity Theory of Beings). This context of good agrees with Plato's definition of good as an object of reason. To Plato knowledge that isn't of the visible world is the highest form of reality; it is the world of reason, the world of ideas and forms. (Gensler, 1998)

Good is relative to the stand point or context of whom or what is asking the question. Good for an animal would be more food, more water, more mates, and more shelter. The human would add material goods and possessions. What then is good for a being? The answer is simply; if more is good for animals more is good for beings. Good for the being is more control, more influence, more knowledge and more awareness.

What is bad?

Once good is understood understanding bad becomes the simple matter of reversing the definition of good. If good is gaining control, influence, knowledge and awareness, then bad is the loss of control, influence, knowledge and awareness. For the animal a loss of food, water, mates, shelter…any item of physical or material want or need would be bad. For a Being, bad would be losing control of actions, the loss of knowledge of how to control actions or just the plain loss of knowledge or awareness of something. This creates a paradox because for a being bad must often occur for good to happen. For example to learn something new a being must frequently replace or discard an old outdated or proved to be false idea with the new one. This bad or discarding of old knowledge must occur in order for good to happen, and can cause the closest thing to real pain a being (separate from the earthly physical being or human) can experience. This is a dilemma that has faced beings for millennia, and has been the cause for many failures in the advancement of humanities body of knowledge.

Better than good

To carry forth the theory of beings model towards our goal of explaining Holiness and leadership, our definitions of good and bad need to be expanded. Basic understanding of good and bad isn't enough when contemplating complex concepts like leadership. The other ethical questions related to good and bad needing elaboration is what is better than good? And what is worse than bad?

Better than good for a being can be the compounding or multiplication of good or the compounding of gaining control, influence, knowledge and awareness. This can be achieved by giving or sharing. Giving knowledge occurs most often and is the most easily recognized form of "better than good". It is done by teachers, parents and by all people that share knowledge. For those sharing knowledge, it influences the actions of each other throughout each day. It's the source of cooperation and group achievement.

The appropriate term for "better than good" in it's purest form matches well with definitions of holy. The definition of Holy or Holiness is often defined as being religiously sanctified, linked or possessing a close connection to god or the Holy Sprit. Holy is frequently associated with scriptures, holy persons, places and events.

Scriptures or holy books and writings impart an ideological or theological knowledge base that influences or dictates (controls) the actions of the followers.

Religiously designated or holy persons are a walking reference guide to scriptures and set a living, visible, example for others to follow.

Places and events exemplify the adage of a picture is worth a thousand words and can also impart knowledge and provide an experience that in turn influences or controls the actions of people. The point is that everything holy in one form or another extends control or imparts knowledge from one being or beings to others.

Gaining of new knowledge often accompanies the relinquishment of old knowledge. The person or being is faced with judging whether to accept the new knowledge or keep the old, whether it is a new method of making coffee or a new way to live your life.

New knowledge gained will influence or change the actions taken by the person accepting the new knowledge by means of becoming the basis on which decisions are made. At the same time the being gaining new knowledge now has new tools to manipulate or control more of their surroundings in the future.

Problems abound around the management of knowledge. One prime example is in schools, the curriculum taught shapes the beings that children grow in to, and will shape and guide (and to a certain extent, control) the behavior of these young adults throughout their entire lives. Its little wonder there is so much debate on the subject.

Governments also use knowledge as a tool to control the behavior. The former Soviet Union and the present North Korea are notorious for going to great lengths to control knowledge available to its people and as much as possible limit or control information that leaves the country.

Knowledge is a tool and a weapon that has been exploited by people and groups for centuries. The earliest big advance was the printing press and has since spread from books and newspaper to radio and television and now to the World Wide Web of the Internet.

Originally knowledge through media was relatively easy to control, printing presses are large complicated machines and expensive to operate. The expansion of media to radio and television had similar constrictions, being large, complicated and expensive to operate. All of these forms of communication were able to be controlled by governments, the elite or the wealthy and there are countless examples of these powers using media to sway public opinion on a whole spectrum of issues from what toothpaste to buy and who gets elected to opinions about other countries and governments.

A common goal in military warfare is air superiority, with air superiority an advisory can go anywhere and do almost anything. A similar situation can be said for controlling the media of a country, by controlling the media a government, group or adversary can do nearly whatever they want and either the population won't know or can be flooded with false information that is taken for the truth.

Holiness associated with religion or bestowed by God is sanctified holiness. Holiness in the context of Relativity Theory of Beings is distinct in that it is holiness by merit or holiness by the act of sharing control, influence, knowledge and awareness with other beings. The remainder of this book when speaking of holy or holiness will be referring to holy of merit. Holiness of merit through teaching is something very special since it can give knowledge and awareness (along with the control gained using that knowledge and awareness) without depleting the source.

Holy persons throughout history have fit the definition of leader and teacher; some are recognized as very great leaders and teachers. (Wright, 1999) The important point here is that all teachers are holy of merit because they devote their lives to the holy act (of merit) of increasing the knowledge and awareness of other beings. Beings gaining knowledge in turn use it to control and influence the world around them.

What is Evil?

Evil is another much debated term, there are many definitions (Tooley, 2002) In keeping with the proceeding definition of holy in context of Relativity Theory of Beings it becomes easier to understand. If one being willingly takes control, influence, knowledge or awareness, from another being that being is committing an evil act. Evil is the intentional taking from another.

Evil is very special because it is easily mistaken for good. It actually fits the definition of good since it increases the material items of an animal or the control, influence, knowledge or awareness of a being. Many evils are committed through ignorance of not understanding evils nature. (Dorter, 1997) The major difference is that the good that the evil being is gaining is at the expense of another being. It is also important to note that the taking has to be intentional and without consent. (Shore, 1995 Nov-Dec) Without evil intent loss at the hands of another being, though certainly bad is not evil. Some may modify the definition of evil to be the taking or destruction of control, influence knowledge or awareness not for personal gain but with the sole purpose to deprive it from another being. The end result for the victim is the same; the simplest resolution to this is to call one evil for gain or selfish evil and the other evil for deprivation or evil destruction. Evil for gain provides the evil doer more resources to carry out evil again but evil for deprivation may seem a "purer" from of evil because no good comes from it for the evil doer.

Evil for deprivation is often a vengeful type of evil, exemplifying an "if I can't have it no-one can" attitude.

When a being dies the control, knowledge, influence and awareness possessed by that being ends. Consciously or subconsciously those present at the moment of death feel that end of life and to a certain extent what made up that being is subsumed by those present. The survivors may then allow that being to a certain extent to live on in them.

The significance of death makes the act of murder exceedingly evil because the murderer causes the loss of life (the end of the being's, control, influence, knowledge and awareness) and is frequently present at the moment of death (which for most that have been present at the death of a loved one is an exceedingly poignant experience that often affects the individual for the rest of their lives).

Forgiveness

Here it is important to note the very special act of forgiveness. Forgiveness is when the victim releases claim of that which was lost. This cuts a tie to the evil one by severing or ending the dispute over the offence. The victim gives to the evil doer that which was taken, and in effect turns the evil act of another into a holy act by the victim. Often times and especially in more egregious crimes the victim does not give the loss to the evil doer but gives the loss to God thereby denying possession of what was taken to the criminal.

Relative Levels of Beings

There is holiness in the interaction or joint action of many beings which creates many levels of beings, each relatively greater or lesser than others, but so unique it is impossible to accurately compare. All beings are relatively different in size and capabilities but are composed of exactly the same elements; control, influence, knowledge and awareness.

Beings are not of the flesh but exert control over flesh. One scale to measure beings is the scale of the biology or physical bodies the being controls. The lowest ends of the scale are microbes and plants that are governed by biology and chemistry. Next there are animals that are certainly influenced by biology and chemistry but are largely controlled by instinct. (Bernard & Mills & Swenson, & Walsh, 2005)

People being of flesh have needs, wants and desires of the flesh and thus are animal like but have learned to control their instincts in order to develop complicated societies and bodies of knowledge. Beyond single bodies, people animals and even some plants, insects and microbes have learned to join forces and willingly share control, influence, knowledge and awareness in order to accomplish greater things than they could have alone. They create a new more powerful and capable being by performing the holy act of joining forces. For example when a couple unites (as in marriage) they share control, influence, knowledge and awareness and between them form a greater being formed through a holy (of merit and often sanctified) union.

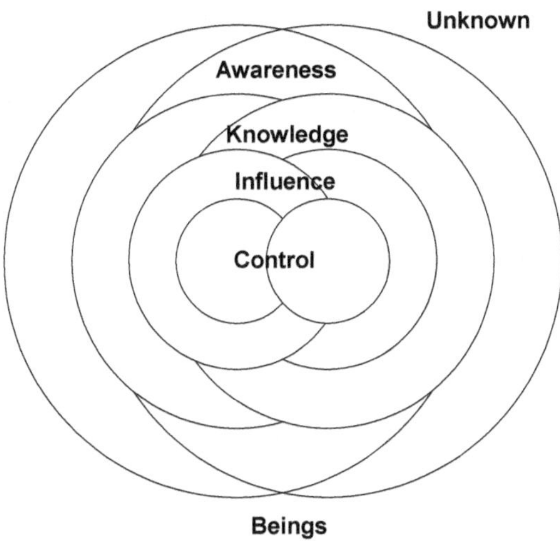

This couple then may raise a family that also shares control, influence, knowledge and awareness. The family then becomes a relatively greater being. The sharing and joining of individual beings to make up greater beings can be short or long term, flexible or rigid. Greater beings extend to; extended families, friends, neighborhoods, communities, municipalities, states and nations each relatively greater than the last. And it doesn't end there; a common element of science fiction is the "earthling" illustrating that someday there will be a relative being encompassing the entire population of the planet earth. Understanding this aspect of the nature of beings makes it easy to understand how opposing nation's competition over control of lands that each has a claim to, sees each other as evil.

Levels of beings can take many forms, every person to some extent is a "multi-being" or part of many different group beings such as; religions, race, ethnicity, economic systems, ideologies, philosophies, sports fans, gender, sexual orientation, as depicted in the following diagram.

gender
sexual orientation
theories
belief
career
occupation
trade
profession
language
culture
creed
national origin
military
community
unions
clubs
political party
alumni
religion
race
ethnicity
economic system
ideology
philosophy
sports fan

People gain a sense of power and worth from belonging or contributing to other beings, and in doing so sacrifices some individual control but they are rewarded by sometimes great power. For example a member of a nation can make war with another nation and a member of a state can execute criminals. Had not the individual beings that comprise the nation or state surrendered or given power, the nation or state would be powerless.

Each relative being, (comprised of individuals that may simultaneously be part of many other relative or group beings) is a real being like many of those we interact with throughout out lives. Relative beings are born, live and die, some even go through the same life stages as people; infancy, childhood, adolescence, adulthood, middle age and old age. With careful observation one can recognize a group being and see that numerous group beings behave very "human" like. Many group or relative beings display the same emotions, reactions and behaviors demonstrated in individual behavior. In some instances it may even prove useful to diagnose group beings with psychological disorders of individuals and craft treatment based on that diagnosis. The challenge is that group beings interact primarily with other group beings and that individuals are largely powerless to communicate or interact with a group being. So treatment of a group being takes action crafted at a scale commensurate with the group being treated, otherwise the action is useless. The best example of two group beings diametrically opposed is war.

Amazingly, almost all group beings are multi-beings just as people are. Community groups, companies, organizations and clubs can be profit or non-profit, public or private. States and Nations can be democracies, monarchies, capitalist or socialist.

One of the most prestigious and sought after group for nations to be in is the "nuclear club" or nations that possess nuclear weapons. The nuclear club is very exclusive and the existing members try very hard to limit the membership.

Every group being whether it be club, community, nation or state, may participate or act in conjunction with other group beings to make a group being made of group beings or a compound multi-being.

Nations are not the ultimate of group beings, groups of people and their leaders have reached the level of Gods. Some religions have had as a core tenant the belief that the adherents are descendant of the Gods that created the earth. (This of course led to problems with neighbors that were believed not to have such a noble lineage). Other societies throughout history have spawned leaders that have called themselves Gods. The pharaohs of Egypt and the rulers of the Aztecs are but two examples. More recently many individuals have called themselves Jesus , Messiah, or messenger of God.

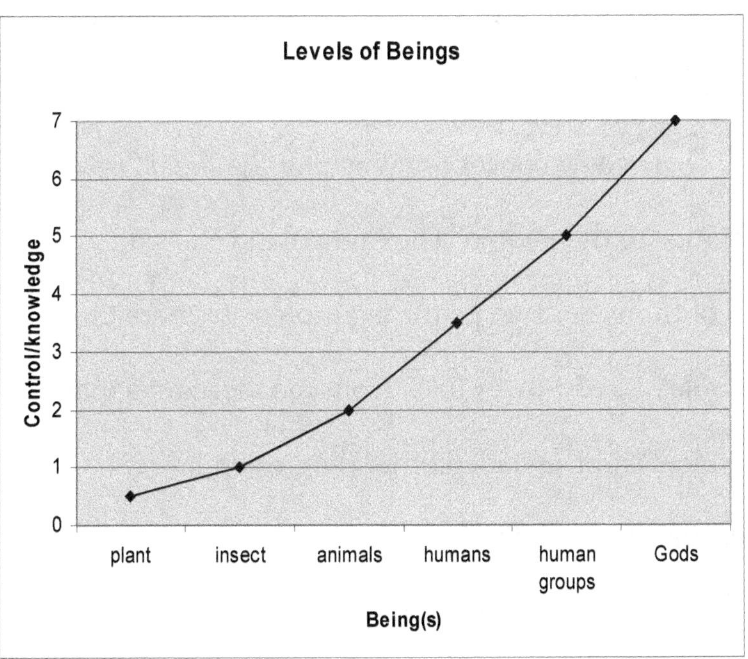

Kings and Queens are somewhat unique in that the people are the subjects or belong to the King or Queen yet Kings and Queens also belong to the people. The subjects claim connection to a King or Queen and the greater the King or Queen the more value or self worth falls to the subjects. The King or Queen owes their authority, power and wealth to the people.

The key concept here is that the "real" power belongs to the people. The French and Russian revolutions are two prime examples of where the people seized power back from the monarchs that had lost sight of the fact that they ruled largely because the people allowed them to.

If something threatens to take away or undermine the sense of control and knowledge from a being it is seen as evil. This impacts everything from sharing of resources of neighboring communities to paradigm shifts within academic theories.

The most famous conflicts between group beings are between religious doctrines. Religious indifferences have been the basis of numerous wars. And countless lives have been lost throughout human history as a result of wars fought because of religious intolerance (Giedl, 2001). Many religions have intractable proclamations that contribute to conflicts. Muslims have the Islamic profession of faith, "There is no God but God, and Muhammad is the messenger of God" (La ilaha illa Allah, wa Muhammadun rasul Allah). (Qamar-Ul, 2003) Judeo-Christians have the First Commandment "I am The Lord your God, Who brought you out of the land of Egypt, out of the house of bondage. You shall have no other gods before Me." (Exodus 20:2-3 RSV).

Today there are many conflicts occurring that can be understood better by using Relativity Theory of Beings. By using Relativity Theory of Beings it becomes easy to understand the point of views between the Arab-Israel conflict; each sees the other as "evil" by trying to take control of land and resources from the other and each possesses ideology that glorifies themselves and condemns the other. Each sees their own actions against the other as righting a wrong or "Just", and sees the other as evil.

Towards the other end of the spectrum, Relativity Theory of Beings can explain why many parents dealing with adolescent children have problems when the children start to exert their independence.

The parents are seen as evil because from the point of view of (or relative to) the teenager they are taking control from the teenager, making the parent "evil". On the other hand parents' sees teenagers as taking control away from the "family" typically lead by the parents.

Group beings are aware that they are made up of individual beings and use this knowledge to mold existing members to tighter alignment with the group's goals and values (making the group being stronger) and to attract new members.

Life Force, Mana and Belief

Control, influence, knowledge and awareness has been defined in this book as the discretionary control that separates higher level beings from lower level creatures such as plants and animals. It's also shown to be fluid and dynamic, it can flow like a river yet be given and taken.

The characteristics of control or power or mana have been equated by many cultures with blood. Blood, to many beings, is believed to have special properties or meanings, and has lead to such practices as blood sacrifice, and blood oaths. The phrase to have a person's blood on their hands reflects this, even though no blood may be literally on the person's hands, the person responsible for another's death often is described as such.

Control influence, knowledge and awareness are bounded by a certain extent by capacity but the biggest boundary for most beings is belief. Bounded control influence, knowledge and awareness can be illustrated with the belief in life force or mana from many oceanic cultures.

Traditional mana is defined as power, influence or authority and is gained by birthright or conquest. In a lighter sense mana is equated to or parallels luck.

Within a culture, if the people believe that power can be attained by birthright it is so. Earlier this book introduced that one of the most basic type of group beings is the one created by the family. The power of the family is often channeled into the children and when the parents or grandparents age and eventually die what was possessed by the ancestors' passes to the new generations. Control, influence, knowledge, and awareness or power or mana is passed from generation to generation.

Life force may also be linked to control, influence knowledge and awareness but is too closely associated with the soul or sprit. The soul and sprit are metaphysical terms most often associated with religions and are viewed as separate entities distinct from the control, influence, knowledge and awareness (or mana) which is viewed here as power that was held by one being and passed or taken by another.

Man is bound by the rules of belief. If a being agrees to follow the rules of mana (or belief) then that being's control, influence, knowledge and awareness is bounded by that belief. Even to the extent of causing physical benefit or harm (and not just in oceanic cultures but also in most religions). There have been many cases of spells or hexes having real effects and many documented cases of the placebo effect in medicine, not to mention many, more cases of answered prayers. All these prayers, spells, hexes and placebos illustrate the power of belief over the being.

Belief in mana is often described as a pre-religion or in other words the power of belief to influence beings is one step away from a true religion. Religions have at their core an independent God or Gods which can be thought of as mana given a life of its own. But basic principle of giving up a portion of ones individual control, influence knowledge and awareness to be bounded or relinquished control to the belief is the same.

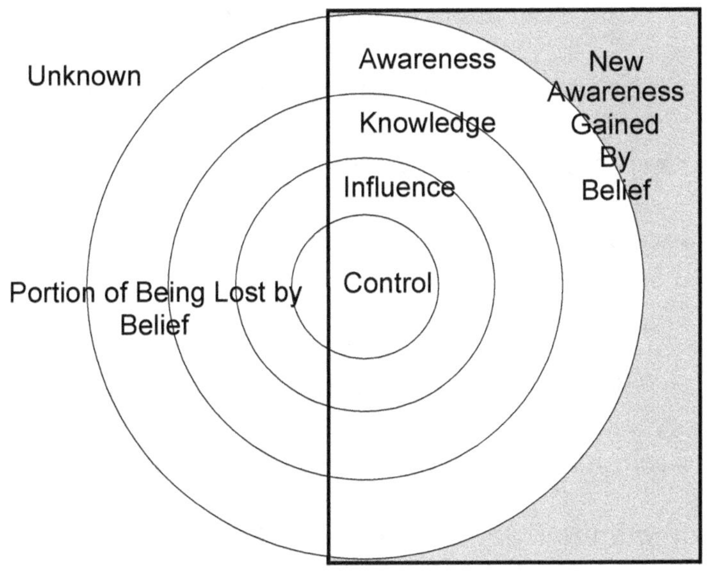

Being bounded by belief

A single believer might look like a much weakened individual because they give up so much of their control. However group being created by the shared belief and the sacrificed control of the individual empowers the group being much more.

Since believers offer up more of themselves compared to most other group beings, a believer group being is much stronger and has greater chance of survival than a group being not based on a strong belief.

Belief need not be restricted to pre-religions and religions. One basic tenant of a group being is shared knowledge and shared belief.

All beings (to some extent) have Knowledge that is factual and can be verified. Belief cannot be verified, but is characterized by the being as knowledge and is treated as true and factual, taking belief up to a level valid enough to base decisions and actions on.

Different beings frequently have conflicting beliefs and behind almost all conflicts are differing belief systems. Many conflicts would simply disappear if belief were replaced by knowledge.

Beings and Technology

Technology has had a great impact on humanity and has also impacted beings. The World Wide Web has enabled beings to share their knowledge among each other in a way that was unprecedented in history, even exceeding the impact of the spread of knowledge facilitated by the invention of the printing press and removable type. Human beings have shown themselves to need to share themselves, and technology has responded with tools to help them do that.

The internet has sites that allow you to load information, pictures and videos of your choosing about yourself. Many people choose to document their entire lives on these web sites. Writers can post their works on sites, electronic bulletin boards, and electronic user submitted documents such as wiki's or discussion forums known as blogs.

People who are interested can create their own virtual beings (player characters) in massive multi-player games that live in virtual worlds on the Internet. These virtual beings in virtual worlds interact with other virtual beings that have at their source "real" people. In these virtual worlds people can achieve greatness in the virtual world in ways that would be impossible in the real world.

The greatness achieved in the virtual worlds is mostly achieved at the expense of non-player characters, these non-player characters are computer generated and have no real person behind them. Many non-player characters perform mundane tasks in the virtual world or are there to be conquered in order to increase the rank or status of the player characters without impacting the status of characters with "real" people behind them.

In the near future real human beings will be able to duplicate themselves in a virtual world that duplicates the real world. This will be a fascinating development since the duplicate beings will use computer generated artificial intelligence to create alternative selves or beings that match the character and personality of the "real" person. The technology is close to the point that it will become difficult to tell the difference between the real person and the artificial person. The truly amazing thing is that the virtual being will be able to outlive the real person and continue to live as long as the virtual world is maintained, human beings will in a sense become immortal in a virtual world.

What will soon be able to be achieved with technology has been in existence since mankind has been able to communicate with each other and form group beings. That is through leadership.

Leadership and Holiness

Holy persons and Leaders have many similarities both, guide, direct and teach. Like religion and holy persons, leaders often develop out of a need, a challenge or a problem that the followers need help getting through or figuring out. (Ryan, 1994)

Many leaders throughout history can be linked to external events that created a hole or vacuum linked to a problem or crisis that a leader was able to step in and solve or be a catalyst of change to overcome or otherwise get past the adversity.

Sometimes leaders create their own crisis by pointing out or convincing a group or groups of people of the existence of a problem or a potential problem.

Leaders and followers identify with each other and define themselves as part of the being created by the leader follower union.

A "Relativity Theory of Beings" definition of leadership or a leader is when a person is able to create a higher level of being by uniting a group of individuals or subgroups behind themselves, a cause, or a body of knowledge. Given that leaders help with overcoming problems and obstacles, the "Relativity Theory of Beings" definition of leader parallels with beings created around philosophies, religions and ideologies.

The link between leadership and holiness is unmistakable. Leadership can come from books like the Holy Bible, Holy Torah and Holy Quran. These Holy works offer guidance on how to handle most of mankind's problems and unite groups of people into higher levels of beings by their shared knowledge, goals and beliefs. When the layperson has trouble finding leadership from the sacred writings religious leaders (priests, rabbis, mullahs, etc.) step in to help. Religions offer the added benefit of divine intervention and the promise of everlasting life.

Leaders can be good, bad, holy or evil. An evil leader would falsely gain control of followers by use of lies deceit or deception and use that control for personal gain or enrichment, or take or deprive control from others.

Truly great leaders are known for teaching or indoctrinating their followers with the leader's goals and knowledge so much so that the leader lives on in their followers (the "being" survives).

When a leader's knowledge and values (what amounts to the leaders controlling forces) are passed on to the followers the life essence or driving force of the being is passed also. The leader's knowledge and values (once incorporated into the recipients being) will stay with and influence the follower from that moment on.

Many great and notorious leaders have initiated movements that have far out lived the leader and exceeded many times over what one person could have ever accomplished in a single life time. This distribution or cascade of the leader's intent is the reason a fear of creating a martyr can be a major concern when deciding the fate of an influential or charismatic individual with a cause. While the leader or holy person is alive there is a certain amount of ownership or control that limits the cause. When the leader dies it not only sets an example for others and raises the worth of the cause (because it is now worth the leader's life) it sets the cause free and may be adapted to other situations by other individuals then passed on to future generations.

Conclusion

Holiness is the ultimate form of leadership. A holy leader helps overcome difficulties and strife while giving of themselves to empower their followers. Holiness is in its purest form is an example of intrinsic good, good for its own sake and that with avoiding evil should serve as a beings noblest purpose for live. Holiness of merit is a wellspring of knowledge that all future generations of mankind can base their decisions on. Holy persons give pieces of themselves to all that they come in contact with and in doing so achieve the realest form of immortality possible.

The question of "What was God's purpose for creating the universe?" best is answered by God. A guess can be made by observing as objectively as possible the universe, its actions and trends.

The universe is in a constant struggle to achieve a balance of all its forces and energy, in a word, to achieve "perfection". The universe is toiling towards the ultimate good, the intrinsic good, Good for its own sake. Mankind as members and elements of the universe should strive to do the same.

REFERENCES

Ayatullah Murtada Mutahhari . (2007, March 12). Goal of Life . *Ahlul Bayt Digital Islamic Library Project*, Ch 4. Retrieved March 12, 2007, from http://al-islam.org/short/goal/

Bernard, L. & Mills M. & Swenson, L. & Walsh, P. . (2005, May). An Evolutionary Theory of Human Motivation. *Genetic, Social, and General Psychology Monographs* , *131*(2), 129-184. Retrieved March 3, 2007, from InfoTrac database.

Buchanan, B.G. . (2006, Winter). What do we know about knowledge?. *AI Magazine*, *27*(4), 35. Retrieved March 3, 2007, from InfoTrac database.

Dorter, K. (1997, December). Virtue, knowledge, and wisdom: bypassing self-control. *The Review of*

Metaphysics, 51(2), 313. Retrieved March 7, 2007, from InfoTrac database.

Edwards, P. (1998, Summer). God and the Philosophers. (from Aristotle to Locke, part1) . *Free Inquiry, 18*(3), p36. Retrieved March 3, 2007, from InfoTrac database.

Feldman, F. (1997, April). On the intrinsic value of pleasures. *Ethics, 107*(3), 448. Retrieved March 3, 2007, from InfoTrac database.

Gardner, S. (2006, September). Sartre, Schelling, and onto-theology. *Religious Studies, 42*(3), 247. Retrieved March 7, 2007, from InfoTrac database.

Gensler, H.J. (1998). Plato. *John Carroll University.* Retrieved March 3, 2007, from http://www.jcu.edu/philosophy/gensler/ms/plato-00.htm

Giedl, L. (2001, November 29). Thou shalt know no god but mine: Religious pride has spawned countless wars of intolerance against other faiths.. *The Christian Science Monitor,* 19. Retrieved March 7, 2007, from InfoTrac database.

Horowitz, T. (1998, January). Philosophical intuitions and psychological theory. *Ethics, 108*(2), 367. Retrieved March 3, 2007, from InfoTrac database.

Johnson, C. . (2000, Winter). Taoist Leadership Ethics. *Journal of Leadership Strudies, 7*(1), 82. Retrieved March 3, 2007, from InfoTrac database.

Luper, S. (2002, May 22). Death. *Stanford Encyclopedia of Philosophy*. Retrieved March 3, 2007, from http://plato.stanford.edu/entries/death/

Miller, B. (1996, August 22). Existence. *Stanford Encyclopedia of Philosophy*. Retrieved March 3,

2007, from http://plato.stanford.edu/entries/existence/

Morley, J. (2005, Fall). The Being of the Phenomenon: Merleau-Ponty's Ontology. *Journal of Phenomenological Psychology, 36*(2), 276. Retrieved March 3, 2007, from InfoTrac database.

Newman, L. (2005, April 14). Descartes' Epistemology . *Stanford Encyclopedia of Philosophy* . Retrieved March 13, 2007, from http://plato.stanford.edu/entries/descartes-epistemology/

Papineau, D. . (1998, January 18). Don't Know Much Biology. *New York Times Online*. Retrieved March 3, 2007, from http://www.nytimes.com/glogin?URI=http://ww

w.nytimes.com/books/98/01/18/reviews/980118.18 papinet.html

Qamar-Ul, H. (2003, June). Knowledge of Allah and the Islamic view of other religions. *Theological Studies, 64*(2), 278. Retrieved March 7, 2007, from InfoTrac database.

Ryan, A. . (1994, Spring). Do we overstate the importance of leadership?. *The Wilson Quarterly, 18*(2), 55. Retrieved March 7, 2007, from InfoTrac database.

Shore, P. (1995 Nov-Dec). The time has come to study the face of evil. *The Humanist, 55*(6), 37. Retrieved March 7, 2007, from InfoTrac database.

Sugden, R. . (2004, January). What public choice and philosophy should not learn from one another. *The American Journal of Economics and Sociology,*

63(1), 207. Retrieved March 7, 2007, from InfoTrac database.

Sullivan, J. (2002, December 19). Plagiarism hysteria lacks original thought. *The Age*. Retrieved March 3, 2007, from http://www.theage.com.au/cgi-bin/bommon/popupPrintArticle.pl?path=articles/2002/12/18/10401

Swierczek, F.W. (1988, November). Culture and training: how do they play away from home?. *Training & Development Journal*, *42*(11), 74. Retrieved March 13, 2007, from InfoTrac database.

Thinkers. (1999, December). Abraham Maslow: the hierarchy of needs. Thinkers. Retrieved March 3, 2007, from InfoTrac database.

Tooley, M. (2002, September 16). The Problem of Evil. *Stanford Encyclopedia of Philosophy* . Retrieved

March 7, 2007, from http://plato.stanford.edu/entries/evil/

Trewavas, A. . (2003, May 9). Aspects of Plant Intelligence. *Oxford Journals Annals of Botany, 92*(1), 1-20. Retrieved March 3, 2007, from http://aob.oxfordjournals.org/cgi/content/full/92/1/1

Wall, S. . (2007, February 13). Perfectionism in Moral and Political Philosophy. *Stanford Encyclopedia of Philosophy* . Retrieved March 3, 2007, from http://plato.stanford.edu/entries/perfectionism-moral/

Wigelsworth, J.R. (2003, December). Lockean essences, political posturing, and John Toland's reading of Isaac Newton's principia . *Canadian Journal of*

History, 38(3), 521. Retrieved March 13, 2007, from InfoTrac database.

Wikipedia. (2007, January 23). Ontology. Wikipedia. Retrieved January 23, 2007, from http://en.wikipedia.org/wiki/Ontology

Wright, D.P. (1999, October). Holiness in Leviticus and Beyond. *Interpretation, 53*(4), 35. Retrieved March 7, 2007, from InfoTrac database.

Zimmerman, M.J. (2002, October 22). Intrinsic vs. Extrinsic Value. *Stanford Encyclopedia of Philosophy*. Retrieved March 3, 2007, from http://plato.stanford.edu/entries/value-intrinsic-extrinsic/

INDEX

www.ingramcontent.com/pod-product-compliance
Lightning Source LLC
LaVergne TN
LVHW020651100826
845148LV00012B/2437